resistance is fertile

compiled summer 2024

the haiku of coffee

coffee bar whimsy
caffeinated, cared for, hugged
id cow and parrot

by
lichen glen

the dedication page bit

this is a small book of verse. please don't view seriously. hopefully some of it will be enjoyed.

curated in space, with time, thank you to Jenny; always:

and to Nicola and James, and Finn and Elsie, for the lovely hospitality, hugs, coffee and deliciously sloppy sandwiches at the cow&parrot, aberfeldy.

and the small but mighty poetry group for the support, encouragement and humour.

haiku

haiku are a distillation of detail into seventeen syllables, three lines, punctuation, and those wonderful gaps between words

these small pieces of poetry try to encapsulate strict windows of interpretation

in this pamphlet part is meant for fun, a momentary distraction. with abstraction

other parts, well, they may try and mean more.

i hope you enjoy.

glen

Index

science haiku

famous scientists in a nutshell, a small nutshell,
probably hazel, definitely not coconut, though some
were definitely a little plural

resistance is fertile

Ohm's law was first used
as a mantra in yoga,
class meditation

zoom zoom

Christian Doppler
was never sure, if he was
coming or going

bring me home

hidden figures Kath,
Johnson was NASA's flightpath,
man made it to moon

leaky helix

15

Franklin's DNA
discovery overlooked,
it was wet and dry

the real jane

Goodall's chimpanzees
tools, language, complexity
Stop! experiments

my apple is bruised

17

Newton's love of trees
gave rise to great theories,
and aspirin use

abstinence

named Albert Einstein
but in beer kellers he was
another einstein Albert?

orbits

Nic Copernicus
his banned heavenly space spheres
just kept on spinning

observation

all seeing lenses
Galileo Galilei
did not fandango

spring break

the base cell defined
Hook compressed, extended, then
sprung to the great fire

evolution

Darwin's origin
meant natural selection,
a pecking order

not ai

Lovelace computed
repeat, loop, repeat, repeat
Ada her honour

ancestry

monk Mendel, and peas
transmitted heredity,
strong genetic traits

the cleaner

25

Pasteur 'risated
curing, vaccinating ills
strap-line 'Heat to Kill'

original psycho

Freud id theory
was not neurosis, but a
super ego dream

transmission

ac not dc
Tesla's arcing coil, sparking
remote, radar, tech

not just light body cars mr ford

PEANUTS! uses for,
Carver made three hundred how's
cultivar of care

marie was no lamb

29

Curie was nobelled,
a radioactive first
in radium al

manhattan tale

no Bohr, but a blast
said electrons can jump one,
quantum mechanic

of mathematica

Turing, Turing, oh
he shortened the war, AI
killed by prejudice

a small point

Hawking, a big bang
fought disease debilitate,
it was a black hole

haiku haiku

seven syllables
of short concise poetry
meant for distraction

yearning

your warmth buries me
i melt, curl, shake fetal fists
wind blown senses clear

imagination

35

javelins of light
riddled pin holes of smeared mist,
washed painted ether

autumn

life watched from behind
frozen plants, glass, hard held breath,
time holds back its song

murmur

they dance, corruscate
crescendo call, pin clouds
drown the absolute

follow the crowd

the herd does return
to drink from the same wellhead,
though incoherent

daybreak

cherry buds kiss, dawns
sparse warmth leaks through ashen boughs,
clean skies draw foresight

child

life, held deep inside
the curl of your finger, taunts
crystal air reeks light

waiting room

the needle sparks fear
spiders sit waiting, hungry,
exams, do they count

lifestyle

i was rattling along
bustling, thinking, barreling,
then i was alone

interest rate

your butter houses
slowly melt, nigh slightest heat,
beware cold markets

nurture

it's an outpouring
to just let go, and to let
consciousness grow

nightmare

45

they did, they whispered
then drifted, so my mind moved,
i've forgotten where

smoke

as smoke, we caress
wrist biting greedy relief,
tracing rough edged truths

stopping

doing the same walk
stopping, waiting, looking, to
where the grass should part

haicoo

49

whimsical haiku
the not so serious themes
intend to tee hee

how to retreat quickly

brave Sir Robin's book
on medieval warfare,
a runaway smash

an ides for a party

Julius Caesar's
bring-own-cutlery orgies
were very short lived

#@&# it

Hippocrates said
he would not swear any oath,
beware paper cuts

travel sick

Captain Cook's spring break
his first Hawaiian beach stay,
was not repeated

passing bye

I waved a hello
and then realized - oh no,
you can't see me here

haiku art

small thumbnail portraits
of famed artists, most were strange,
not in a bad way

but a needed way
or they could not have been so
extraordinary

Edvard created an outcry

Munch to scream about
modern angst, anxiety,
expensive pastels

Julia Cameron, photographic pioneer

intense still portraits,
enhanced by each scratch and flaw,
she liked to shoot men

Edmonia Lewis, neoclassical sculptress

rarest black swan, her
work marked Cleopatra's grave,
thankfully salvaged

it's surreal Salvador

Dali for a while,
melt watches, blast landscapes, it
was just not normal

carved from a bigger statue

Michaelangelo
how? the hand! each: distinct: view:
three years with david

Amrita Sher-Gil, still life cut short

silent images
interpret all India,
penetrate the heart

Andy's abstraction

oh Warhol is me
pope of pop celebrity,
the art of money

enigma Edward

hollow core Hopper
trapped in limbo, by despair
a limitless space

Clara Peeters, dutch master

defied all odds, each
breakfast piece challenged Rubens,
her reflected self

Claude every hour of the day

not the Monet, or
pretension to understand,
it's simply to love

Merisi's death of the virgin

Caravaggio
expert with light, dark and knife
a basket of fruit

Joseph's year without a summer

Turner erupted
from great impressions, to Boot,
oh sunny Norham

haily individual

69

people of some note
some are off key, some will chime
but the all made waved

Diogenes had Plato over a barrel

gold adulterer
who threw away all possessions,
moved god out of light

Li Ching Yuen, died aged 256

71

had twenty four wives
herbalist, qigong master,
kept a quiet heart

Lord Timothy Dexter, luckiest investor

even shipped fur gloves
for sale in the West Indies,
met cold wind trader

James Barry, c-section first

73

soldier surgeon
pioneered army health care,
was born Margaret

Nils Bolin, saved millions

volvo engineer
gave three point patent away,
seatbelts safe for all

Henry Dunant, first nobel peace prize winner

had twelve nations sign
first Geneva Convention,
formed the Red Cross

James Harrison, donated blood 1,173 times

his blood cures Rhesus
antibody saves unborn,
the golden armed man

Shirley Chisholm, first black congresswoman

granny gave her strength,
always unbought and unbossed,
showed up, stood up, spoke

Alfred Russel Wallace, posted ideas to darwin

sent Darwin thesis
Darwin quickly wrote theory,
Wallace lost the vote

the bit before the end

songs that just don't end
they fold, twist, shape, escalate
just Sound and Vision

the end

81

so there it is, all,
small but fun, joyful, i hope
one of them made you ...

about the author

'Glen' has been a long term creator of words, stories, rhymes and fictions.

A life change three years ago gave the opportunity to write more and look back at older work. Some of it was not that good, some was reasonable and some gave the spark to this book. tThat and good coffee venues.

Haiku wasn't an intended discipline, but I've dabbled. The more recent attraction was distillation, bottling an idea into so few letters, where a comma, can make so much difference to the weight of meaning.

I hope this book provides the enjoyment and fun i have had in writing it.

Best wishes

Printed by Lichen Glen
ISBN: 978-1-0687640-1-1

lichenglen@protonmail.com

www.ingramcontent.com/pod-product-compliance
Lightning Source LLC
Chambersburg PA
CBHW061041050726
47592CB00004B/1542